T4-ABN-747

Main Dishes
RECIPE SAMPLER

*From the
AMISH-COUNTRY
COOKBOOK
Series*

EVANGEL PUBLISHING HOUSE
NAPPANEE, INDIANA

MAIN DISHES Recipe Sampler

Evangel Publishing House
2000 Evangel Way, P.O. Box 189
Nappanee, IN 46550
Toll-free Order line: (800) 253-9315
Web-site: www.evangelpublishing.com

Cover Art: Susan Yoder

ISBN: 1-928915-07-8

Printed in the United States of America
10 9 8 7 6 5 4 3 2 1

Bob and Sue Miller grew up in a small Amish community in Sugarcreek, Ohio. Christian teaching and good home cooking were part of their upbringing, a heritage which continued when they established their own home. In 1971, the Millers opened Das Dutchman Essenhaus, a six-day Amish restaurant in Middlebury, Indiana, complete with Amish and Mennonite cooks and wait-staff.

After enjoying a memorable dining experience, many guests asked about the unique recipes prepared in the Essenhaus kitchens. The Millers responded with a set of three cookbooks containing their own original recipes and others gathered from their employees.

The resulting three-volume series of *AMISH-COUNTRY COOKBOOKS* has sold more than 500,000 copies since Volume 1 was introduced in 1979. In 2000, six "sampler" mini-cookbooks were created, using recipes chosen from the larger three-volume set:

- *Snacks & Appetizers*
- *Breads & Soups*
- *Salads & Vegetables*
- *Main Dishes*
- *Cookies*
- *Desserts*

To order additional "sampler" mini-cookbooks or the full-size *AMISH-COUNTRY COOKBOOKS*, contact your local bookstore or gift store. Or you may contact Evangel Publishing House directly. An order form is enclosed at the back of this book.

CONTENTS

Index to Recipe Location in the AMISH-COUNTRY COOKBOOK Series

Bachelor's Surprise

2 lbs. ground beef
4 cups minute rice
1/2 cup diced onion
salt and pepper to taste
1 can pork and beans

1 can stewed tomatoes
1/2 cup diced green beans
Optional: dash of catsup, mustard,
    Tabasco® sauce
grated cheese

Brown beef. Cook rice. Combine all ingredients and season to taste. Simmer 1/2 hour. When ready to serve, add grated cheese.

Serves 4 to 5 people, or 1 bachelor for a week.

Jon Helmuth, host/waiter

Wan Q Chow Mein

2 tbsp. peanut oil
1 clove garlic, minced
6 oz. thinly sliced beef, tenderloin,
    or chicken breast
1 1/2 cups celery, sliced
1/2 cup water chestnuts, sliced
    thinly
1/2 cup Chinese pea pods, sliced
    thinly lengthwise

1/2 cup carrots, shredded
1 cup bamboo shoots, shredded
1 tsp. salt
2 tbsp. soy sauce
1 tsp. sherry
1 cup chicken broth
1 tbsp. cornstarch
1/2 cup water
hot cooked rice

Heat oil in skillet or wok. Add garlic and meat and quickly brown. Remove meat and set aside. Add celery, water chestnuts, peas, carrots, bamboo shoots, salt and soy sauce. Cook and stir until vegetables are tender but crisp. Add sherry and broth. Cover and bring to a boil. Mix cornstarch with water and add to broth. Cook until slightly thickened. Serve with rice.

4 servings.

Mary Arlene Bontrager, waitress

Baked Chuck Roast

3 to 5 lb. beef roast
1 pkg. onion soup mix
12 oz. cola drink

Place unseasoned roast in baking dish. Sprinkle with onion soup mix. Pour cola drink over roast. Cover and seal tightly with aluminum foil. Bake at 300° for 3 1/2 hours or until tender. This has an excellent flavor.

Edna Nissley, waitress

Go often to the house of your friends,
for weeds choke up the unused path.

Veggie Pizza

2 cups Bisquick®
1/2 cup water
8 oz. cream cheese
2 tsp. horseradish
1/2 cup chopped onion, or 1 tbsp.
   minced onion

1 small can shrimp (may substitute
   tuna, crab, or chicken)
1/2 cup mayonnaise

Mix Bisquick and water. Press into ungreased jelly roll pan and bake 10 minutes at 450°. Cool 20 minutes.

Mix the remaining ingredients with mixer. Spread over cooled crust.

Top with raw vegetables and cheese. I use radishes, broccoli, cauliflower, sliced olives, carrots, celery, and shredded cheese. Pat gently.

Janet Mast

Beef Sausage

1 lb. ground beef
1/4 tsp. nutmeg
1/4 tsp. sugar

1 tsp. salt (scant)
1/4 tsp. sage

Mix well. Shape into patties and fry.

Marsha Gingerich, bakery

What goes into your mind
comes out of your mouth.

Tuna Casserole

2 cans tuna
1 can cheddar cheese soup
1 small onion, chopped
1 can cream of mushroom soup

12 oz. frozen peas
1 lb. bag noodles, cooked and
   drained
1 1/2 lbs. cheddar cheese, shredded

Mix all ingredients except noodles and cheese, then stir in cooked noodles. Pour half the mixture into a 9"x13" dish. Cover with half the cheese, then repeat layers. Bake at 350° for 1 hour. Serves 6-8.

Frances Blough, waitress

Lord, when we are wrong, make us willing to change.
And when we are right, make us easy to live with.

Burritos

2 lbs. hamburger
1 tbsp. seasoned salt
1 tsp. red pepper
3 cans refried beans
1/2 cup chopped tomatoes
1/2 cup chopped green pepper

1/2 cup chopped onion
2 pkgs. flour tortillas
1 quart pizza sauce
1 can nacho cheese sauce
8 slices Velveeta® cheese
1 pkg. mozzarella cheese, shredded

Brown hamburger with salt and red pepper; drain. Add refried beans, chopped tomatoes, peppers, and onions; mix well. Spread mixture on each flour tortilla. Roll up the shells and place in a greased baking pan. Mix pizza sauce and nacho cheese sauce and spread over burritos.

Bake at 400° until sauce bubbles. Spread Velveeta cheese slices and mozzarella cheese over the top. Return to oven until cheese melts. Good with cottage cheese or sour cream and taco sauce.

Martha Miller, dishwasher

Supper Sandwich Bake

12 slices bread
butter or margarine
1 lb. lean ground beef
1/4 cup catsup
1 tsp. salt

6 frankfurters
2 medium onions, sliced
6 slices American cheese
2 beaten eggs
1 cup milk

Spread six slices bread with butter; arrange in bottom of greased 9"x13" pan. Toast in moderate oven (350°) about 15 minutes.

Combine beef, catsup, and salt and spread over toast (1/3 cup per sandwich). Top with frankfurters cut almost in half lengthwise, onion, cheese slices, and remaining bread. Combine eggs and milk; pour over bread. Bake in moderate oven about 50 minutes.

Makes 6 servings.

Debbie Oesch, waitress

Calico Beans

1 large can pork and beans
1 can kidney beans
1 can butter beans
1/4 to 1/2 lb. bacon
1 lb. ground beef or sausage
1 medium onion, diced

1/2 cup brown sugar
1/2 cup catsup
2 tbsp. vinegar
1/2 tsp. salt
optional: 10 oz. frozen lima beans

Drain kidney and butter beans, saving the liquid. In skillet, brown bacon, ground beef and onion. Combine all 3 cans of beans with browned ingredients. Arrange in greased baking pan. Combine brown sugar, catsup, vinegar and salt into a sauce. pour over ingredients in baking pan. If dish is too dry, add some of the liquid saved from the beans.

Bake in 350° oven for 1 hour.

Barbara Bontrager, cashier
Rosa Borntrager, Dutch Country Gifts

Stromboli

Thaw one loaf of frozen bread dough. Roll out to fit pizza pan. Spread pizza sauce over dough. Cover with one layer each:

shaved ham
salami
pepperoni

Sprinkle on mozzarella cheese, Parmesan cheese, and oregano. Roll up like a jelly roll. Stick toothpicks in top to hold dough together as it bakes. Be sure both ends are tucked shut tight. Brush with 1 beaten egg. Sprinkle with Parmesan cheese and oregano. Bake at 325° for 40-45 minutes.

Note: Any meat or vegetable may be used.

Arlene Miller, waitress

Casserole

3 lbs. hamburger
3 onions, chopped
3 cups potatoes, cubed
3 cups celery, sliced
3 cups carrots, diced
3 cans peas

3 cups spaghetti, cooked and
drained
2 cans cream of mushroom soup
9 slices bacon
1 quart tomato juice
1 lb. cheese, shredded

Brown hamburger and onion. Cook vegetables and drain.

In a roaster, place hamburger, vegetables, and spaghetti. Pour mushroom soup over top. Fry bacon and lay over top. Pour tomato juice over all. Sprinkle with cheese.

Bake 1 1/2 hours in a 350° oven.

Amanda Troyer, waitress

Spinach Lasagna

9 lasagna noodles
2 pkg. (10 oz. *ea.*) frozen chopped
   spinach
1 lb. cottage cheese
1 egg, beaten
1 tsp. salt

dash of pepper and garlic
1/4 tsp. oregano
1/4 tsp. basil
10 oz. Monterey Jack cheese
cream (sweet or sour)

Cook noodles and steam spinach until limp. Mix cottage cheese with egg and spices. Layer into buttered 2 qt. baking dish, starting with noodles and ending with cheese. Spread cream on top to keep moist. Bake at 350° for 1/2 hour, covered, and 15 minutes, uncovered.

Julianna Bontrager, waitress

Chipped Beef Casserole

1/4 lb. chipped beef, cut up
2 hard-boiled eggs, diced
1 cup milk
2 tbsp. grated onion
1 cup uncooked elbow macaroni

1 cup condensed cream of
  mushroom soup
1/2 lb. or 2 cups grated cheddar
  cheese

Mix all ingredients and pour into 1 1/2 to 2 qt. casserole dish. Cover and refrigerate overnight. Bake, uncovered, at 350° for 30 minutes or until hot.
Makes 4 to 6 servings.

Edna Fern Schmucker, pie baker

Spamburgers

1 can Spam®
1/2 lb. cheese
1 small onion
3 tbsp. catsup

3 tbsp. milk
2 tbsp. mayonnaise
2 tbsp. pickle relish

Grind Spam, cheese, and onion through food chopper; mix thoroughly. Add catsup, milk, mayonnaise and pickle relish. Spread on buns, wrap in foil, and bake at 300° for about 20 minutes.

Laura Bontrager, bakery

Church Supper Lasagna

13 oz. lasagna noodles
2 tbsp. oil
1 lb. ground beef
2 tbsp. instant minced onion
1/4 cup chopped celery
2 tbsp. chopped parsley
1/4 tsp. garlic powder
1 1/2 tsp. salt
3 cans (8 oz. ea.) tomato sauce
4 sliced hard-boiled eggs
1 lb. sliced mozzarella cheese
16 oz. large curd cottage cheese

Cook noodles; rinse under cold water and drain. Heat oil and brown beef in large skillet. Stir in onion, celery, parsley, garlic powder, salt and tomato sauce. Cover and simmer 15 minutes. Reserve a few egg slices for garnish.

In 9"x13" greased pan, layer about 1/3 each of the noodles, mozzarella cheese, cottage cheese, eggs and meat sauce. Repeat layers twice, ending with meat sauce. Bake in 350° oven for 30 minutes. Garnish with egg slices.

Makes 10-12 servings.

Mary Arlene Bontrager, waitress

Seafood Pasta

1/2 cup butter
2 cloves garlic
8 tsp. flour
1/2 cup Half & Half*
2 to 3 cups milk
2 cans minced clams

8 oz. noodles, cooked and drained
2 cans medium shrimp, drained
2 cans crab meat, drained
basil, to taste
parsley, to taste
lemon juice (opt.)

Melt butter; add garlic. Mix in flour; add Half & Half. Slowly add milk, stirring until thick. Add clams with juice. Mix to medium consistency. Add noodles, shrimp, crab, basil, parsley, and lemon juice to taste.

Yield: 10-12 servings.

Katie Hochstedler, bakery

*Half & Half is a dairy product consisting of half milk, half cream.

Dad's Favorite Steak

Chill a beef top round steak, Swiss steak, or arm roast. Cut 1 1/2" to 1 3/4" thick. Score both sides in diamond pattern. Make marinade:

1/2 cup water	1/2 cup soy sauce
1/4 cup salad oil	1/4 cup lemon juice
2 tbsp. brown sugar	1/2 tsp. ginger
1 clove garlic, minced	10 drops hot sauce

Combine in saucepan and cook slowly for 10 minutes. Chill. Place steak in a plastic bag, add marinade, press out air, tie securely, and place in pan in refrigerator for 6 to 8 hours or overnight.

Remove steak from marinade, reserving marinade, and place on grill over ash-covered coals or on a rack in broiling pan so surface meat is 4" to 5" from heat. Broil at moderate temperature rare or medium (25 to 30 minutes, depending on thickness of steak and doneness desired), brushing with marinade and turning occasionally. Carve in thin slices, diagonally against the grain.

Dick Carpenter, material handling

Salmon Zucchini

1 can (14 oz.) salmon, drained and
flaked
4 tbsp. grated Parmesan cheese
1 cup mayonnaise

2 1/2 cups grated zucchini
1 cup fine dried bread crumbs
2 tbsp. lemon juice

Blend all ingredients, reserving a small amount of the Parmesan cheese
for the top. Spoon into a 2 quart greased casserole. Sprinkle with reserved
cheese. Bake at 350° for 30 minutes.

Serves 6-8.

Emma B. Miller, hostess/cashier

Deep Dish Taco Squares

1/2 lb. ground beef
1/2 cup sour cream
1/3 cup mayonnaise
1/2 cup shredded cheddar cheese
1 tbsp. chopped onion

1 cup Bisquick®
1/4 cup cold water
1 or 2 medium tomatoes,
   thinly sliced
1/2 cup chopped green pepper

Heat oven to 375°. Grease square baking dish 8"x8"x2". Cook and stir ground beef until brown; drain. Mix sour cream, mayonnaise, cheese, and onion; reserve. Mix baking mix and water until soft dough forms. Pat in pan, pressing dough 1/2" up on sides.

Layer beef, tomatoes, and green peppers in pan. Spoon sour cream mixture over top. Sprinkle with paprika if desired. Bake until edges of dough are light brown, 25-30 minutes.

Cheryl Troyer, gift shop, Susanna Miller, cook
Laura Bontrager, bakery, Esther Hershberger

Rosy Cheese Bake

3 eggs, beaten slightly
2 cans (8 oz. *ea.*) tomato sauce
1 cup milk
1 tsp. salt

1/4 tsp. pepper
8 slices bread
1/2 lb. American cheese, grated

Mix eggs, tomato sauce, milk, and seasonings. Arrange alternate layers of bread, cheese, and sauce in greased square pan. Place pan over hot water and bake in a slow over (325°) for 50 minutes or until knife inserted in center comes out clean.

Ida Weaver, cook

Easy Homemade Pizza

Pizza Dough:
4 cups flour
6 tsp. baking powder
2 tsp. salt
1 1/3 cups milk
2/3 cup oil

Pizza Sauce:
4 (6 oz.) cans tomato paste
2/3 cup oil
2/3 cup water
2 tsp. oregano
1 tsp. garlic powder
1 tsp. salt
1 tsp. pepper

In bowl combine flour, baking powder, and salt. Combine milk and oil and pour over flour mixture. Mix with fork, shape into ball, and knead until smooth. Roll out on greased cookie sheet.

Mix all pizza sauce ingredients. Spread on top of crust and add toppings of choice: hamburger, cheese, sausage, onions, green peppers. Bake at 400° for 20-25 minutes. Makes 3 round pizzas.

Polly Yoder, cook

Quickie Casserole

Grease a glass baking dish with margarine and crush 4 cups soda crackers into it. Add a can of tuna and a can of peas, drained. Moisten with enough milk to soften crackers and bake until hot—delicious!

A small child can complete this alone.

Edna Schrock, cook

Sitting still and wishing
Makes no person great.
The good Lord sends the fishing
But you must dig the bait!

Goulash

4 cups macaroni
1 quart tomato juice
1 pint catsup

2 lbs. hamburger fried with salt
    and pepper and a little onion
1/4 cup brown sugar

Heat water to a boil; add 1 tsp. salt. Cook macaroni over low heat till done, stirring occasionally. Put in a 4-quart casserole dish; add remaining ingredients. Mix and bake at 350° for 1/2 hour or till done.

Optional: You may add stewed tomatoes if you like.

Lydia Ann Miller, head cook

Make-Ahead Potatoes

12 large potatoes, boiled in salt
    water and peeled
8 oz. sour cream
8 oz. cream cheese, softened

1 tsp. onion powder
1/4 cup margarine, melted
paprika to taste

Combine cooked potatoes, sour cream, cream cheese, and onion powder and whip or mash until fluffy. Add small amount of milk if necessary. Spread in a buttered 9"x13" pan and refrigerate or freeze until needed.

When ready to use, drizzle melted margarine over top and sprinkle with paprika. Bake at 350° for 1 hour. Delicious with any meat. No gravy needed.

Edna Nissley, waitress

Haystacks

1/2 lb. soda crackers, crushed
2 cups cooked rice
2 heads lettuce, chopped
2 pkg. corn chips
6-8 diced tomatoes
chopped nuts

sliced olives
3 lbs. hamburger, browned
1 jar spaghetti sauce, heated
2 cans cheddar cheese soup, mixed
    with 1 soup can milk, heated

Layer all ingredients on plate in order given.
Serves 12-14 people.

Edna E. Bontrager, cook
Rosa Borntrager, Dutch Country Gifts

Grandma's Dumplings

1 can (14 oz.) chicken broth
1 can cream of celery soup
1 1/4 cups water
2 tbsp. butter or margarine
1 egg

3/4 cup milk
1 1/2 cups all-purpose flour
1 1/4 tsp. baking powder
1 tsp. dried parsley flakes
1/2 tsp. salt

In a 5-quart Dutch oven or heavy saucepan over medium heat, stir broth, soup, water, and butter until smooth. Bring to a boil. Reduce heat to low and simmer. Meanwhile, in a liquid measuring cup beat egg. Add enough milk to measure 1 cup. Combine flour, baking powder, parsley, and salt. Stir in egg mixture just until flour is moistened. (Dough will be soft and sticky.) Drop dough by spoonfuls into simmering liquid. Cover and let simmer for 10 minutes.

Anna M. Slabaugh, bakery

Hobo Dinner

Place a cabbage leaf on a piece of aluminum foil 12"x12". Have the foil large enough so you can wrap up your meal.

On cabbage leaf put a 6 oz. hamburger patty, sliced or shredded potatoes, sliced carrots, chopped onion, salt and pepper to taste. Add 1 slice of Velveeta® cheese and cover with another small cabbage leaf. Wrap tightly in foil.

These can be baked or they can be cooked on a grill if you are camping. Be sure to turn them every 15-20 minutes. It takes at least an hour to cook these on an open fire, depending on how hot the fire. It's best not to cook them on a very hot fire to keep them from scorching. If you bake them in the oven, bake approximately 1 hour at 350°.

Mary Esther Miller, gifts supervisor

Fireside Supper

1 pkg. (7 1/4 oz.) macaroni and cheese

2 cups chopped cooked ham, turkey, or chicken

1 pkg. (10 oz.) frozen peas and carrots, cooked and drained

1 cup dairy sour cream

1/4 cup chopped onion

1 tbsp. chopped parsley

1/4 tsp. rosemary

dash pepper

Prepare macaroni as directed on package. Add remaining ingredients; mix well. Heat thoroughly, stirring occasionally.

6 servings.

Sue Miller, manager

Meat Loaf

2 lbs. ground beef
2 eggs
1 1/2 cups dry bread crumbs
3/4 cup catsup
1 tsp. Accent®

1/2 cup warm water
1 pkg. onion soup mix
2 strips bacon
1 can (6 oz.) tomato paste

Mix all ingredients except bacon and tomato paste thoroughly. Put into loaf pans. Cover with bacon. Pour tomato paste over top. Bake for 1 hour at 350°.

Katie Miller, gift shop

Swallow your pride occasionally.
It's not fattening.

Fettuccine Alfredo with Crab

1/2 cup butter, melted
1/2 cup heavy cream
1/3 cup shredded mozzarella
cheese
1 tsp. chopped parsley

1 pkg. imitation crab meat, chunk
style
3 cups cooked fettuccine noodles
parsley, for garnish
1/4 cup Parmesan cheese

Combine butter, cream, and mozzarella cheese and cook over low heat until cheese melts and cream bubbles and thickens. Add parsley and crab. Stir and heat until meat is heated through.

Arrange fettuccine noodles on a large plate or shallow dish. Pour mixture over noodles and garnish with parsley and Parmesan cheese. Serve at once.

Serves 4.

Malinda Eash, Knot 'n' Grain

Oven Barbecued Steaks

3 lbs. round steak, cut 3/4" thick
2 tbsp. vegetable oil
1/2 cup chopped onion
3/4 cup catsup
1/2 cup vinegar
1/8 tsp. black pepper

3/4 cup water
1 tbsp. brown sugar
1 tbsp. prepared mustard
1 tbsp. Worcestershire sauce
1/2 tsp. salt

Preheat oven to 350°. Cut steak into ten equal portions. Pour oil into skillet, browning each piece of steak on both sides. Transfer steak to a roasting pan. Add onion to oil in skillet and brown lightly. Add rest of ingredients to make barbecue sauce and simmer for 5 minutes. Pour sauce over steaks in pan. Cover. Bake 2 hours, or until meat is tender.

Martha Miller, cook

Egg Rolls

1 lb. sausage
2-3 large cloves garlic, minced
1 onion
1/2 head cabbage, shredded
1 tsp. salt

1 handful bean sprouts
1/2 tsp. pepper
egg roll wrappers (2 dozen)

Fry sausage, garlic, and onion. Add cabbage, salt, bean sprouts, and pepper and heat briefly. Wrap in egg roll wrappers and cook, following directions on back of package. This makes approximately 2 dozen egg rolls.

For sauce: Saute 2 large cloves garlic, minced in 2 tbsp. oil. Add 3 tbsp. catsup and 1 tbsp sugar.

Alice Golden, waitress

Pizza Casserole

2 lbs. hamburger
1 cup chopped onion
2 cups macaroni, cooked
    and drained
1 pint (16 oz.) pizza sauce

1 can mushroom soup
2 cups mozzarella cheese, shredded
pepperoni, if desired

Brown hamburger with onion. Add all other ingredients except cheese and mix well. Put 1/2 of mixture in baking dish, add 1 cup cheese, then repeat. Bake at 350° for 30 minutes.

Serves 8-10.

Denise Henke, waitress
Doris Miller, waitress

Cornmeal Mush

4 1/2 cups cornmeal
3 cups cold water
2 1/2 tsp. salt

6 cups boiling water
3 cups milk

Mix cornmeal, cold water, and salt. Stir into boiling water and milk. Bring to boil while stirring. Turn heat to low and cook about 45 minutes, slowly. Stir occasionally. Pour into loaf pans. To keep the top soft, let margarine melt on top of the mush. Lay a sheet of waxed paper over pans to cool.

Slice and fry cold mush in butter until golden brown. Serve with butter and syrup.

Ida Weaver, waitress

Poor Man's Steak

1 lb. hamburger
1 cup milk
1/4 tsp. pepper
1 cup cracker crumbs
1 tsp. salt

1 small onion, finely chopped
1 can mushroom soup, diluted
    with 1 soup can water

Combine all ingredients except mushroom soup. Mix well and press in cookie sheet. Refrigerate for at least 8 hours or overnight.

Cut into squares, roll in flour and brown in skillet. Put slices in layers in a roaster, spreading mushroom soup on each piece. Bake at 325° for 1 hour.

Sue Miller, manager
Lizzie Ann Bontrager, cook

Chili Egg Puff

10 eggs
1 tsp. baking powder
1 pint creamed cottage cheese
1/2 cup butter or margarine
1/2 cup flour

1/2 tsp. salt
1 lb. shredded cheese
2 (4 oz.) cans diced green chilies

Combine all ingredients. Heat and pour into a 9"x13" pan. Bake at 350°
for 35 minutes. Serves 10 to 12. Good with salsa.

Viola Miller

When God measures men, he puts the tape
around the heart and not the head.

Reuben Casserole

1 jar (32 oz.) sauerkraut, drained
2 medium tomatoes, sliced thin
2 tbsp. Thousand Island dressing
butter as desired
4 pkg. sliced corn beef

2 cups shredded Swiss cheese
1 can (10 oz.) refrigerated biscuits
Optional: 2 rye crackers, crushed
1/4 tsp. caraway seeds

In a 9"x13" pan, spread sauerkraut, arrange tomato slices, spread with dressing, and dot with butter. Cover with corned beef and cheese. Separate each biscuit into 3 thin layers and arrange over casserole. Sprinkle with crumbs and caraway seeds.

Bake at 425° for 10 minutes or until biscuits are golden.

Edna Hochstetler, crafts

Cheese Soufflé

8 slices bread
1 lb cheese, grated
1/4 cup margarine
cubed ham, bacon, or mushrooms
6 eggs, beaten

2 cups milk
1 tbsp. onion salt
salt
pepper

Cube bread and put in bottom of casserole. Combine cheese, margarine, and meat. Sprinkle over bread cubes. Mix eggs, milk, and seasonings. Pour over top of casserole. Refrigerate overnight. Bake at 325° for 45 minutes.

Esther Nisley, pie baker

Six Layer Dinner

1 lb. ground beef
1 cup onion, sliced
1 cup celery, sliced
2 cups carrots, sliced
2 cups potatoes, sliced

salt
1 can cream of chicken or celery
   soup
1/2 soup can water

Place meat in bottom of casserole. Add remaining ingredients in order given. Salt each layer. Mix soup and water and pour over top. Cover casserole and bake 1 1/2 hours at 350°.

Barbara Bainter, cleaning service

Experience is a wonderful thing. It enables you
to recognize a mistake when you make it again.

Broccoli and Ham Pot Pie

1 pkg. (10 oz.) frozen broccoli,
    cooked and drained
2 cups ham, cooked and cubed
3 tbsp. chopped onion
2 cups Swiss cheese, shredded

1 (10") pastry shell
1 1/4 cups Half & Half*
3 eggs, slightly beaten
salt and pepper to taste

Mix first 4 ingredients and place in pastry shell. Scald Half & Half and add eggs. Pour over vegetables and meat. Bake at 350° for approximately 45 minutes or until brown on top.

Amanda Miller, bakery

*Half & Half is a dairy product consisting of half milk, half cream.

Spanish Rice

Melt 2 tbsp. butter in frying pan. Add:

1/2 cup dry rice	1 onion, minced
1/2 cup green pepper	1/2-3/4 lb. ground beef

Let brown until rice is lightly browned and the meat golden, stirring to prevent over-browning in spots. Add:

1 cup water	1/2 tsp. celery salt
3/4 tsp. salt	1/8 tsp. pepper
1 can tomatoes	

Let simmer slowly until all the liquid is absorbed and the rice is tender, about 30 minutes.

Betty Schrock, cakes

Breakfast Pizza

1 pkg. (8) refrigerated crescent rolls
   or homemade pizza dough
1 lb. bulk pork sausage
1 cup frozen hash browns

1 cup shredded cheddar cheese
5 eggs, beaten with 1/4 cup milk,
   1/2 tsp. salt, 1/8 tsp. pepper

Place crescent rolls or pizza dough in 12" pizza pan to form crust. Brown sausage and spoon on crust. Sprinkle with potatoes, top with cheese, and pour egg mixture over all. Bake at 375° for 25-30 minutes.

Makes 6-8 servings.

Rosa Borntrager, Dutch Country Gifts
Lyle Coblentz, dishwasher

Sweet and Sour Beef

2 lbs. beef
4 green peppers, cut in strips
4 stalks celery, coarsely chopped
2/3 cup onion, chopped

Meat Marinade:
1/2 cup vegetable oil
4 tsp. cornstarch
4 tsp. red wine
8 tsp. sugar
8 tsp. soy sauce

Mix marinade ingredients and pour over beef. Cover and refrigerate overnight or longer.

In covered skillet over medium high heat, heat meat and marinade to boiling. Reduce heat and simmer 30 minutes, or until meat is fork tender, stirring occasionally. With slotted spoon, remove meat and set aside.

To skillet, add peppers, celery and onion. Cover and cook over medium heat until tender and crisp.

Wilma Weaver, waitress

Baked Potatoes

1/2 lb. bacon
9 boiled potatoes, mashed,
  seasoned with milk, salt and
  pepper, and butter
1 medium onion, finely chopped

3 eggs, beaten
3 tbsp. grated Parmesan cheese
1 pkg. (8 oz.) cheddar cheese,
  grated

Fry bacon, drain, and dice. Mix all ingredients thoroughly; place in casserole and top with buttered crumbs and parsley. Bake at 350° till golden brown.

Serves 6 to 8.

Barbara Bontrager, cashier

Taco Pie

1 unbaked pie shell
1 lb. hamburger
1 medium onion, chopped
1/2 pkg. taco seasoning
water

1/2 cup sour cream
4 oz. shredded cheddar cheese
shredded lettuce
1/2 cup crushed taco chips

Brown hamburger with onion; drain. Add taco seasoning and enough water to moisten. Put mixture into crust. Top with sour cream and cheese. Bake at 375° for 20-25 minutes. Top with lettuce and taco chips and serve.

Elma Miller, waitress

Baked Potato Wedges

5 or 6 potatoes, scrubbed and cut
    into wedges
2 tbsp. Parmesan cheese
1 tsp. salt
1/2 tsp. pepper

1/2 tsp. garlic powder
1/2 tsp. paprika
1/2 cup oil

Arrange potato wedges skin side down in shallow baking pan. Mix remaining ingredients together and brush or pour over potatoes.

Bake at 375° for 45 minutes.

Alice Risser, Dutch Country Gifts cashier

Baked Chicken

chicken pieces
1 1/2 cups sour cream
1 tsp. Worcestershire sauce
2 tsp. celery salt
dash garlic salt

2 tbsp. lemon juice
1/2 tsp. paprika
1 tsp. salt
bread crumbs

Mix all ingredients together except chicken pieces and bread crumbs. Rinse chicken pieces and pat dry. Roll in sour cream mixture, then in bread crumbs. Bake at 375° till done.

Mary Ellen Campbell, waitress

If you can't forgive others, you have burned the bridge over which you must pass.

Baked Beans

2 lbs. navy beans
1 tbsp. salt
1/2 lb. bacon

1 small onion
1 1/2 cups brown sugar
1 quart tomato juice

Wash beans and place in a large cooking pan twice the size of the amount of beans. Fill pan with cold water and allow beans to soak overnight. In the morning, add salt and simmer approximately 2 hours, or until tender. You may need to add 1 cup water in the second hour.

Cut up and brown bacon with chopped onion. Add bacon with 2 tbsp. drippings, brown sugar, and tomato juice to beans and place in baking pan. Bake 3-4 hours at 350°. Cover for about half the baking time. You may add hot dogs the last 30 minutes of baking.

Rosa Borntrager, Dutch Country Gifts

Chicken and Dressing

1/2 cup milk
3 cups herb-seasoned croutons
1/2 cup celery, diced
1 tbsp. minced onion
3 cups cooked chicken
3 eggs, beaten
1 can cream of chicken soup
1 cup milk

1 tsp. salt
1/2 tsp. poultry seasoning
1/2 tsp. marjoram flakes
1/2 cup flour
1/4 cup Parmesan cheese
1/4 cup butter
1/2 cup almonds

Pour 1/2 cup milk in greased 9"x13" pan. Combine croutons, celery, and onion. Spread in dish. Sprinkle chicken over croutons. Combine eggs, soup, 1 cup milk, salt, poultry seasoning and marjoram. Pour over chicken.

Combine flour, cheese, and butter, blending until crumbs form. Sprinkle over casserole, top with almonds.

Bake at 375° for 40 minutes.

Esther Hershberger

Spicy Chicken Gumbo

1/4 cup oil
2 cloves garlic, minced
2 onions, diced
1 green pepper, diced
2 tbsp. flour
2 1/2 cups cooked tomatoes
2/3 cup tomato paste
1 1/2 tbsp. salt

1 1/2 tbsp. Worcestershire sauce
1/2 tsp. chili powder
1 bay leaf
2 cups cooked okra (or celery)
3 cups broth or stock
1/4 tsp. pepper
1/8 tsp. ground cloves
pinch dried basil

In a large heavy kettle, saute garlic, onions, and green pepper in oil. Blend in flour. Cook and stir over low heat until vegetables are tender, then add rest of vegetables and seasonings. Simmer for 1 hour.

Prepare cooked rice to serve 8: Saute 2 cups rice (white or brown) in enough oil to coat kernels evenly for 5 to 10 minutes. Add 4 cups water and simmer until tender and all the water is absorbed. Add 2-3 cups cooked chicken to gumbo. Simmer briefly. Remove by leaf. To serve, mound rice in center of soup bowls. Sprinkle with parsley.

Carolyn Mast, waitress

Chicken and Spaghetti Casserole

1 - 5 or 6 lb. chicken
salt to taste
1 lg. pkg. spaghetti
2 or 3 onions
2 or 3 green peppers

1 lb. canned chili without beans
1 can tomatoes
1 can (8 1/2 oz.) mushrooms
1 lb. grated cheese

Cook chicken in water, seasoning with salt to taste. When well done, cool slightly and pick from bone; cut in bite-size pieces. Use 2/3 of broth to cook spaghetti; do not rinse. Chop onions and peppers and cook in remainder of broth until tender.

In a large buttered roasting pan, layer half the chicken, half the spaghetti, and half of the onions and green peppers with juice. Spoon over half the chili, half the tomatoes, half the mushrooms, and half the grated cheese. Add second layer the same way. Cover with foil and bake for at least 2 hours at 325°. Add water if needed.

This makes a good dish for a carry-in meal.

Leora V. Kauffman, purchasing

Savory Crescent Chicken Squares

3 oz. pkg. cream cheese, softened
3 tbsp. butter
2 cups cooked chicken, cubed
1/4 tsp. salt
1/8 tsp. pepper

2 tbsp. milk
1 tbsp. chopped pimento
8 oz. can crescent rolls
3/4 cup seasoned croutons,
   crushed

Preheat oven to 350°. Blend cream cheese and 2 tbsp. butter until smooth. Add the next 5 ingredients, mix well. Separate crescent dough into 4 rectangles. Firmly press perforations to seal. Spoon 1/2 cup meat mixture into center of each rectangle. Put 4 corners of dough to top center of chicken mixture, twist slightly, and seal edges. Brush top with reserved 1 tbsp. butter and dip in crouton crumbs. Bake on ungreased cookie sheet 20-25 minutes until golden brown.

Make mushroom sauce: heat together 1 can mushroom soup and 1/2 to 1 cup milk. Serve with chicken squares.

Lavera Hooley, waitress

Chicken Bar-B-Q

2 1/3 to 3 1/2 lbs. chicken
1 cup catsup
1/2 tsp. pepper
1 medium onion, finely chopped
1/2 cup margarine

1 tsp. salt
1/4 tsp. garlic salt
1 tbsp. Worcestershire sauce
1/3 cup lemon juice or vinegar

Mix catsup, pepper, onion, margarine, salt, and garlic salt in a saucepan and bring to a boil. Remove from heat and stir in Worcestershire sauce and lemon juice. Pour over chicken and roast, covered tightly, for 2 hours or until tender.

Fannie Yoder, cook

Fruited Chicken

3/4 cup sifted flour
1/4 tsp. garlic salt
1/4 tsp. ground nutmeg
1/4 tsp. salt
1/4 tsp. celery salt
2 1/2 to 3 lbs. chicken pieces

1/2 cup butter or margarine
2 (20 oz.) cans pineapple chunks in
   heavy syrup
3 tbsp. flour
1/3 cup soy sauce

In a plastic bag, mix 3/4 cup flour and seasonings. Add chicken pieces, a few at a time. Shake to coat. Brown chicken in margarine, reserving drippings. Place chicken pieces in a 9"x13" baking dish.

Drain fruit, reserving 1 1/2 cups syrup. Arrange fruit over chicken. In saucepan, stir together 3 tbsp. flour and fried chicken drippings. Add 1 1/2 cups syrup and 1/3 cup soy sauce. Stir until thickened and bubbly. Spoon over chicken. Cover with foil. Bake at 350° for 1 hour.

Serves 8.

Anne Yoder, restaurant manager

Chicken Cacciatore (Crockpot)

1 large onion, sliced
2 1/2 to 3 lbs. cut-up fryer chicken
2 (6 oz.) cans tomato paste
1 tsp. salt
1 clove garlic, minced
1/2 tsp. basil

1 bay leaf
1 can (4 oz.) drained mushrooms
1/4 tsp. pepper
1 to 2 tsp. oregano
1/2 tsp. celery salt

Place onion in crockpot. Add chicken. Mix remaining ingredients and pour over chicken. Cook on low for 7 to 9 hours or high for 3 to 4 hours. Good served over hot buttered spaghetti. May also be cooked in the oven.

Betty Graber, waitress

Chicken Divan

3/4 lb. boned, skinned chicken
2 tsp. oil
1 cup water
1 tbsp. dry sherry wine
1 pkg. (10 oz.) frozen broccoli

1 can (10 3/4 oz.) condensed cream
   of chicken soup
1 1/2 cups instant rice
1 tbsp. grated Parmesan cheese

Brown chicken in oil, stirring occasionally. Add water, wine, broccoli, and soup. Bring to a full boil. Separate broccoli pieces. Stir in rice, cover. Remove from heat and let stand 5 minutes. Sprinkle with cheese.

Makes 4 servings.

Patty Kauffman, grill worker

ORDER FORM

Name _____

Address _____

City _____ St._____ ZIP Code _____

Qty	Title	Price Ea.	Total
	Salads & Appetizers Recipe Sampler	5.99	
	Breads & Soups Recipe Sampler	5.99	
	Salads & Vegetables Recipe Sampler	5.99	
	Main Dishes Recipe Sampler	5.99	
	Cookies Recipe Sampler	5.99	
	Desserts Recipe Sampler	5.99	
	Amish-Country Cookbook - Volume I	12.99	
	Amish-Country Cookbook - Volume II	12.99	
	Amish-Country Cookbook - Volume III	12.99	
		SUBTOTAL	
		Indiana Residents add 5% tax	
		Postage & Handling (10% of Subtotal; $1.50 minimum)	
		TOTAL	

Please see the other side of this form for Payment and Mailing Information.

PAYMENT INFORMATION

☐ **Check/Money Order Enclosed**
Make check or money order payable to "Evangel Publishing House"

☐ **VISA**   ☐ **MasterCard**

Card No. _____ / _____ / _____ / _____

Expiration Date: _____ / _____

Name (as it appears on card): _____

Card holder's signature: _____

Mail this order form and your payment (in U.S. funds) to:
Evangel Publishing House
P.O. Box 189
Nappanee, IN 46550

Visit our website: www.evangelpublishing.com
or use our toll-free Order Line: 1-800-253-9315 (between 8:00 a.m.-4:30 p.m. EST)